Bring Lent to Life

Activities & Reflections for Your Family

Kathleen M. Basi

Liguori

Imprimi Potest:
Harry Grile, CSsR, Provincial
Denver Province, The Redemptorists

Published by Liguori Publications
Liguori, Missouri 63057

To order, call 800-325-9521
www.liguori.org

Library of Congress Cataloging-in-Publication Data

Basi, Kathleen M.
Bring Lent to life: activities and reflections for your family / Kathleen M. Basi.—1st ed.
    p. cm.
ISBN 978-0-7648-2004-5
1. Lent. 2. Families—Religious life. I. Title.
BV85.B36 2011
263'.92—dc23

                                                                2011030541

Liguori Publications, a nonprofit corporation, is an apostolate of the Redemptorists. To learn more about the Redemptorists, visit Redemptorists.com.

Printed in the United States of America
17 16 15 14 13 12 11 / 5 4 3 2

Contents

Resources

Devine, Arthur. "Prayer of Quiet." The *Catholic Encyclopedia*. Vol. 12. New York: Robert Appleton Company, 1911. 8 Feb. 2011 <http://www.newadvent.org/cathen/12608b.htm>.

The Little Ways. "How to Make Sacrifice Beads." http://thelittleways.com/how-to-make-sacrifice-beads ©2004–2008.

INTRODUCTION

Lent:
The Misunderstood Season

I have a confession to make. Are you ready? OK, here goes: I love Lent.

Whew! Now with that out of the way—and now that I have exposed myself as a true Catholic geek and you've all thrown the book across the room (and hopefully retrieved it)—I'll move on to why.

Lent is a season of contrasts. During Lent, we prepare to celebrate the memorial of Christ's passion, death, and resurrection—the centerpiece of our Christian faith. During this season, we focus on fasting, almsgiving, and prayer. But mostly we focus on giving things up and how unpleasant that can be. Am I right?

This is also the time of year when Earth hurtles through its miraculous odyssey of rebirth. At the start of the season, stark winter holds sway, but by its end, all the Earth glories in an explosion of color.

Lent is a journey from death to life, both spiritually and in the physical world. On Ash Wednesday, we strip the liturgy of its alleluias. We strip the sanctuary to its most basic elements. The Church asks us to come away to the "desert," away from distractions and, in the simplicity of the season, to be renewed.

We are sinners, and we always will be, but penitence is not a destination. "Repent" is a call to action, an attitude that points toward reconciliation, toward holiness, toward renewal—in short, toward Easter. Even the dramatic, emotionally draining liturgies on Holy Thursday and Good Friday crackle with anticipation of the resurrection. In the midst of the "Great Fast," there is plenty of room for joy. We don't have to spend the entire forty days focusing on misery.

Speaking of "forty," let's talk about that number. At some point during every Lent, most people say, "Forty? Is that all it is? It sure *feels* longer than forty days!"

Guess what? It is. The period of time from Ash Wednesday to Easter Sunday actually includes 46 days. Technically, Sundays don't fall within the fast. And technically, Lent ends on Wednesday of Holy Week. Triduum is its own fast.

But to the vast majority of us who are not liturgy geeks, Lent includes the whole works. So rather than getting stuck on the number forty, let's resolve to do as a wise man once advised me: to think of "forty" in the biblical (that is, symbolic) sense. And that is?

A really long time.

This Lent, let's journey together through some of the most important elements of our Christian faith. Let's explore them like children, with our children.

How to Use This Book

The section titled "Getting Ready" introduces two activities that anchor the season and provide us with a visible measure of our progress toward Easter: the Easter Tree—a bare tree to which we will add leaves and flowers as the season progresses—and Sunday Love Letters.

Following those pages, we begin a week-by-week breakdown of the season of Lent. Each week we will zero in on one aspect of our Lenten journey.

- From Ash Wednesday throughout the first week of Lent, we will explore the three pillars of Lenten observance: **fasting, almsgiving, and prayer**.
- In the second week, we will talk about **baptism and the RCIA**.
- In week three, we'll do some spiritual spring cleaning and focus on **reconciliation and repentance**.
- Week four we devote to the journey from death to life, which is echoed in the **renewal** of nature all around us.
- In week five, we will begin our countdown to Easter, walking step by step through the **passion**, using the tradition of "Easter story eggs."
- Finally, we arrive at **Holy Week** and the great Triduum celebration that culminates in Easter, the most important day of the year.

Each week begins with general information on the topic to help parents "unpack" our faith in preparation for sharing it with our children. This is followed by specific reflections for both adults and children. Periodically, you will find sections to read to your children. These are set off for easy identification.

At the end of each week are a series of activities ranging from day trips to crafts to cooking, including recipes. The last activities in each week are connected with the Easter Tree. Please remember that it's not necessary to do every activity listed. Lent is a long season, and trying to do something every day will burn out the entire family. Each week, choose a few activities or reflections that are appropriate for your family.

At the end of the book are two appendixes. Appendix A offers suggestions for celebrating major feasts that fall during the season. Appendix B has the patterns needed for the Easter Tree.

Of the two major Christian seasons, Lent/Easter is the one that slips under the secular radar—and that's a good thing. Easter is the most important celebration of the Christian year. But because our culture doesn't really know what to do with it, Lent offers us a yearly opportunity to renew our faith, unencumbered by secular distractions.

This year, let us commit ourselves to embrace the total meaning of Lent in all its beauty. Let us commit ourselves to journey through the desert...and to be renewed.

GETTING READY

Creating Your Easter Tree

In *Joy to the World: Advent Activities for Your Family* (Liguori Publications), I used the Advent calendar as a countdown to Christmas. Lent is a little harder, because it's about dying to self rather than celebration and anticipation. Besides, it's just so long! Young children often have a hard time processing the length of one week, let alone six and a half.

So we won't do a day-by-day countdown during Lent. But we will create a visual "calendar" of sorts by creating an Easter Tree.

To make the Easter Tree:
- Find a large dead branch and plant it in a pot, OR
- Draw and color a bare tree on two pieces of poster board taped together, and then mount it on the wall.

During the season, you will need:
- The flower and leaf patterns in Appendix B (or you can make your own)
- Construction paper in spring colors
- Scissors
- Tape

If you are using the wall mural, you will need:

- Tape or stick tack to attach leaves and flowers to the mural

If you are using a branch, you will need:

- A hole punch and string to hang the leaves
- Plastic straws

Using the patterns in Appendix B, make leaves and flowers (with stems!) in various shapes and colors. Keep them in a box where children can access them easily. As Lent unfolds, you will use the Easter Tree in many ways. Each day, you will place leaves on the tree and flowers at its base for prayer requests, for moments of thanksgiving, and in response to reflections. If you are using a potted branch, you can wrap plastic straws in green construction paper and tape the flowers to them. Then they can be stuck into the pot around the base of the tree.

If you have pre-reading children, it would be a good idea to designate a flower type or color for different kinds of prayer—for instance, tulips for intentions, daisies for prayers of thanks, leaves for weekly reflections. By the time Lent is over, your Easter Tree will have transformed from a bare, dead skeleton to a bright spring mural filled with the prayers and thoughts of the season.

This is our Easter Tree. Right now, at the beginning of Lent, its branches are bare—just like the trees outside. During Lent, we will add leaves and flowers to it every day. Sometimes we will add them as part of an activity as we talk about different parts of our faith. But any time you are thankful for something or have someone you want to pray for, make a leaf and put it on the tree.

Sunday Love Letters

Over the course of the next few weeks, we're going to do many different things to help us grow in our faith. During the week, we'll talk about praying, fasting, giving alms, and other aspects of our Lenten journey. We'll read reflections, we'll do activities, we'll add to our Easter Tree.

But Sundays are for love letters.

It's really hard to tell people how important they are to us. It makes us uncomfortable to open ourselves up that way. For that matter, it makes us uncomfortable to receive such praise. And yet doing so is powerful and very important.

If you think about it, Sunday itself is like a love letter from God to humanity. On this day of rest, which God made for us (Mark 2:27), we gather to break open the Word through Scripture and the Eucharist. And in so doing, we open ourselves to the message of divine love.

What better way to carry our Sunday worship into the world than to nourish the core relationships in our lives? On the Sundays of Lent, we focus on renewing relationships by having each family member write a note to another family member, a different one each week. In larger families, it might be a good idea to set up some sort of rotation at the beginning of the season to ensure that everyone gets a letter every week. Small families may run out of immediate family members to write to before the season ends; if so, expand your sights to include grandparents, aunts, uncles, cousins, even friends and clergy members. We all need affirmation.

What goes in a love letter? Here are a few suggestions:

- Words of affirmation. Consider these notes a chance to turn negative attitudes into opportunities to build one another up.
- Gratitude. Thank loved ones for specific things they have done and times in which they have helped you.
- Blessings and prayers.
- Apologies. This can be the place to address unresolved hurts.
- Ways in which others have blessed you.
- Reflections. Tell others how you see God reflected in them.
- Love! Simply tell others how much you love them.

Some family relationships are inevitably more strained than others. Use this activity to heal broken relationships as well as strengthen healthy ones.

Notes don't have to be long or well written; they just need to be sincere. Even pre-reading/writing children can participate. They may need help from a parent or an older sibling. Ask them what kinds of things they like to do with the person they are writing to; they may even need prompting to call experiences to mind. But once they find what is in their heart, children are very creative with artwork. They can evoke a concept through pictures and explain it to the recipient.

It's going to take a certain level of commitment to ensure this happens every week. It will be all too easy to set it aside in favor of other activities. You might consider devoting half an hour before or after Mass to write and exchange notes. Or perhaps you can write them and leave them on the family member's pillow to be read at bedtime.

As we will see in the coming weeks, Lent is about far more than sackcloth and ashes. Lent gives us the yearly gift of renewal. Embrace it by renewing the relationships in your own family.

For the Children

Every Sunday in Lent, we're going to write a note to (or draw a picture for) a different person in our family to tell them what we love about them. How does this person help you to know God better? What is your favorite thing about the person? Sometimes this is going to be hard because family members get angry at one another. But it's important to do it anyway, because it will help us love one another better.

LENT

ASH WEDNESDAY

Fasting and Almsgiving

A man used to go into his local watering hole every night and order three drinks. When people asked him, "Why do you order three drinks?" he would answer, "Oh, I have two brothers who live far away. When we parted ways, we promised that wherever we were, we would always drink together."

Then one night the man walked into the bar and ordered only two drinks. Shocked and sympathetic, the locals patted his shoulder and offered their condolences on the loss of his brother.

"Oh, no, it's nothing like that," he said cheerfully. "You see, it's Lent, and I quit drinking."

When a priest friend of mine heard this story, he laughed for ten minutes. Then he said, "That is a perfect illustration of how *not* to do Lent!"

Isn't this the temptation we all face? After the excess of Christmas, we have a respite of a few weeks, and then we plunge into the gray, gloomy heart of Lent. We know we're supposed to give something up...but why, exactly?

For the Children

Jesus spent forty days in the desert, fasting and praying, to help him get ready for his public ministry. We call this a "retreat." But most of us can't take that much time to get away and pray. Lent gives us a chance to do a month-long retreat in the middle of our ordinary lives.

Choosing a penance to observe throughout the season keeps us from forgetting that we are on retreat. But faced with the prospect of piling deprivation on top of late-winter blues, it's tempting to make Lenten penance as painless as possible. On the other hand, good old Catholic guilt is always ready to offer the opposite idea: Lent should be good and hard. We *should* be miserable during Lent. Offer it up!

Well, there's value in that. But really, the best path lies somewhere in the middle.

Reflections

Fasting

The problem with simply giving something up is what I call the Mardi Gras syndrome: You're sacrificing sweets for Lent, so the day before Ash Wednesday you have four bowls of ice cream. (There's a reason it's called "fat Tuesday.") And on Easter Sunday you celebrate the end of the fast with two chocolate bunnies, a couple dozen handfuls of jelly beans, three slices of pie, and a cinnamon roll.

Kind of misses the point of the fast, don't you think?

Fasting should change us in some way—move us to a place of greater holiness. It shouldn't be something we do to torment ourselves for a while, only to revert to our former selves when it's all over.

I believe it's time to think beyond the ordinary Lenten penance. Why not give up a specific sin instead? In many ways, sin is a habit, a pattern of behavior. Selfishness, irritability, unkind words, gossip, gluttony—each of us struggles with the same sins again and again. Instead of choosing a specific item to forgo, why not choose one sin particularly troublesome to you and spend Lent focused on breaking its power over you?

This can be a great exercise for kids too, although they may need help, and that help must be given carefully. It's important that we, the parents, not tell children what sins we think they need to address. True conversion happens from the inside out; it cannot be imposed by authority, however loving.

Penance, when heartfelt, is frequently a very private action and very difficult for people to share, even with those closest to them. Respect this. If a child is unwilling to share what he or she is giving up, that's OK. As a parent, it's tempting to feel that we must know everything our children are up to. But it's also possible that a child (especially in the teen years) may want to be free of a habitual sin but is too afraid to admit it to his or her parents for fear of punishment. If your children are sincere enough to choose to work on something for Lent, rejoice, and allow them the freedom to make good choices of their own volition.

It's also important to add that there is nothing wrong with giving up something physical—a literal fast. A family that fasts from an item has a chance to grow in faith and in community. Our family, for instance, gives up sweets every Lent. That is a tradition, and a hard one. That is all we have asked of our small children. But older children can and should choose a Lenten penance unique to their own needs. As you pray and discern your penance in the days and weeks leading up to Ash Wednesday, be sure to encourage your children to do likewise.

Almsgiving

So you've chosen something to give up. Done, ready for Lent! Not so fast. We've forgotten an important point: Lent is not just about fasting. It's also about almsgiving.

Fasting offers us a slowed pace, one that helps us really be aware of how many blessings we take for granted. When we acknowledge the extent of the bounty we have been given, charity flows naturally. Almsgiving is the best way of showing gratitude for all God has given us. It also mirrors Christ's sacrifice in some small way. While fasting is about giving something up, almsgiving is about *doing* something.

Prayer with fasting is good. Almsgiving with righteousness is better than wealth with wickedness.

TOBIT 12:8

Almsgiving, in its most literal sense, means charity. The world is full of those who need charity, and there are plenty of ways to help meet those needs. Around 13,000 parishes in America participate each year in Catholic Relief Services' Operation Rice Bowl. In this program, families simplify their meals and donate the savings to the hungry.

When I was growing up, every night during Lent my mother would put a quarter under each family member's plate. These quarters were squeezed from the family's grocery budget. Every night after the meal prayer, we placed the coins in the rice bowl, giving us a tactile connection to the act of almsgiving. At the end of the season, we put those coins in an envelope and dropped them in the collection basket at church.

Another possibility would be to collect money in a jar on the table and then carry it to a local food pantry or shelter. This brings the lesson closer to home and gives the family a chance to interact directly with those less fortunate.

Feeding the hungry is a terrific Lenten practice. But almsgiving is more than just money. As the prophet Isaiah puts it:

Is this not, rather, the fast that I choose:
releasing those bound unjustly,
untying the thongs of the yoke;
Setting free the oppressed,
breaking off every yoke?
Is it not sharing your bread with the hungry,
bringing the afflicted and the homeless into your house;
Clothing the naked when you see them,
and not turning your back on your own flesh?

ISAIAH 58:6–7

Perhaps this year you can find a new way to serve the needy: volunteer at a soup kitchen, a food bank, or a secondhand clothing store. Work with a local St. Vincent De Paul chapter. Or perhaps you can start even closer to home.

Lent is about right relationship with God. What better way to grow closer to God than getting into right relationship with those closest to you? Use this time to renew relationships with loved ones: spouse, parent, sibling, child. In choosing your Lenten penance and discipline, find a way to serve, to heal broken relationships, to die to self. Is there some act of service you can perform quietly, without fanfare or fuss, for someone you love? Young siblings who fight over toys can vow to yield;

a spouse can commit to acts of service he or she wouldn't ordinarily perform.

Think this is a cop-out? Think again. This is hard stuff. I'm suggesting that we subordinate our ego, that we empty ourselves as Christ did on the cross. After all, those we interact with every day are the body of Christ, and when we serve them, we serve God.

For the Children

During Lent, we try to get closer to God by doing two things. One is called fasting. Fasting is when we give up something we like, such as candy or TV. Fasting can also be when we give up a sinful habit, like whining or tattling on people.

The other thing we do during Lent is called almsgiving. Even though we're not rich people, we have so much more than we need. We take it for granted sometimes, but there are lots of people in the world who don't have enough. Almsgiving is when we take some of what we have and give it to the poor. During Lent, we are going to eat a little less, a little less fancy, which will save a little money. We'll put this money in a container (rice bowl), and at the end of Lent, we'll give it to people who don't have enough to eat.

Activities

Attend Ash Wednesday Mass as a family. Be sure to explain why we are signed with ashes; don't let this be something you do "just because," something cool and mysterious but ultimately without meaning.

For the Children

Today is Ash Wednesday. It's called that because at church the priest or another minister will draw a cross on our forehead with ashes. The ashes are what is left when last year's Palm Sunday branches were burned. We use them because a long time ago, whenever people were sorry they had hurt God, they would take off their normal clothes and put on sackcloth and sit in ashes. It reminded them—and it reminds us—that God made us out of dust, and when we die, our bodies will become dust again. It is God whom we want to please, and God whom we hurt every time we sin.

Choose a Lenten penance. You will need paper and pencils or crayons, a fireplace or fire pit, and matches.

For the Children

Sin is when we choose to do things God asks us not to do. Sin puts up a wall between us and God. Everybody sins every day. Usually, we commit the same sins over and over. God wants us to love him and to love one another. When we argue with our brother or sister, when we take toys or refuse to share, when we say mean things about people, it makes God unhappy. Can you think of something you do that makes God unhappy? Will you give it up for Lent? Write it down or draw it on a piece of paper.

After everyone in the family has written down what they are going to do for Lent—and remember, family members should have the freedom to keep their goals private—fold the pieces of paper and burn them.

Remember how we got ashes on our foreheads to remind us that our sins hurt God? Well, another thing that happens when we burn something is that the ashes blow away in the wind. That's the way God is with our sins: as soon as we let them go, so does he. God forgives us. That's why the prophet Isaiah said, "Though your sins be like scarlet, they may become white as snow; Though they be red like crimson, they may become white as wool" (1:18).

So today we're going to take these pieces of paper and burn them to symbolize our sins burning up, gone forever, once we repent.

Make sacrifice beads. Saint Thérèse of Lisieux had a set of beads on which she counted the sacrifices she offered up to God. "Sacrifice beads" are a string of ten beads, plus an "Our Father bead," which can be used as a rosary as well as counting good deeds. They are small enough to fit in a pocket. Inexpensive sets can be found online by searching for "sacrifice beads" or "Saint Thérèse Beads." If desired, you can also make them as a family craft project (see instructions at http://thelittleways .com/how-to-make-sacrifice-beads. This could be a great way to help family members carry out their Lenten commitments.

Make pretzels. If you think fasting is hard on Ash Wednesday and Good Friday, take comfort. In the early centuries of the Church, fasting was serious business. In many parts of the world, the faithful were called to fast from all animal products (including fat, eggs, and milk) for the entire Lenten season. Pretzels—a food made without these ingredients—developed in response. According to one tradition, the shape we know today was meant to symbolize arms crossed in prayer.

Since we are no longer prohibited from eating animal products during Lent, you can choose whatever recipe you like best to make your own pretzels. A simple recipe and directions can be found on page 27.

For the Children

During Lent a long time ago, everyone fasted from meat, eggs, milk, and even butter. It must have been hard to find food that tasted good. A monk came up with a special bread that he twisted into the shape of folded arms, which was how people used to pray. They called this new snack "bracellae," which means "little arms" in Latin. The Germans turned that name into "bretzel," which eventually became "pretzel."

Your Easter Tree

Choose a Lenten "resolution." Jesus says that any time we serve others, we serve him. Sometimes this is hard to do. There are people we don't like very much, and sometimes we even have confrontations or arguments with people we love. But Jesus lives in each one of us. He wants us to love one another and serve one another.

Think of someone you have trouble getting along with and resolve to do something small for that person every day during Lent. Children may need help with their resolution. Suggest that they get a classmate's lunch box for him, make their sister's bed for her, or clean their room without being asked.

On an Easter Tree leaf, write down the person's name or draw a picture of him or her. Then write down or draw something you can do for that person. It doesn't have to be the same thing every day—just something small and quick to show you love the person.

After everyone has chosen a Lenten resolution and drawn a picture on a leaf, have each family member hang his or her leaf on your Easter Tree.

Recipe

Pretzels

Free of dairy and eggs, pretzels originated during the days of stricter Lenten fasts. This recipe accompanies the activity on page 24.

1½ cups warm water

1½ tsp. active dry yeast

2 T. brown sugar

1⅛ tsp. salt

2 T. slightly melted butter (too hot and it will kill the yeast)

4 cups flour

2 cups warm water

2 T. baking soda

Dissolve yeast in 1½ cups warm water. Add brown sugar, salt, and butter to yeast mixture and stir to dissolve.

Add flour to mixture; knead dough until smooth and elastic. Let rise for ½ hour.

While dough is rising, prepare a "soda bath": mix 2 cups warm water with 2 T. baking soda.

When dough is ready, pinch off sections and roll into long ropes about 15 inches long and ½-inch in diameter. Shape into folded arms as shown on page 28. You'll have to show your children how to fold the first one, but be sure to let them do as much of the work as possible.

Dip pretzels in soda bath. This gives them a glossier texture. (You can also use an egg wash.) Place on a greased baking sheet.

Let the pretzels rise again, but not for too long or they will lose the characteristic holes upon baking. Bake at 450 for 10 minutes.

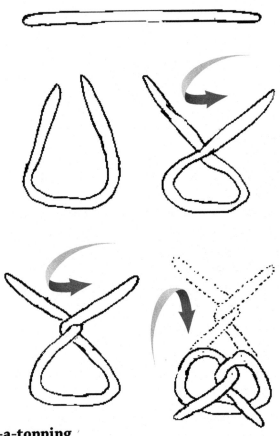

Pick-a-topping

Melt 4 T. melted butter (to help other toppings stick) and brush over pretzels. Top with or roll in:

- Kosher or sea salt
- Cinnamon sugar (¼ cup sugar, 4 tsp. cinnamon)
- Seeds (sesame, poppy, sunflower)
- Melted cheese and bacon bits
- Icing glaze

LENT

FIRST WEEK

Prayer

Two thousand years ago, Saint Paul urged the Thessalonians to "pray without ceasing." Unfortunately, over the passage of twenty centuries, we've lost sight of his original meaning. The word *prayer* evokes an image of people on their knees, hands folded, eyes closed, talking to a God who takes requests like a genie in a lamp and zaps them into reality here on Earth.

There is no such thing as unanswered prayer, but sometimes the answer is "not yet" and sometimes "no." Prayer is not about changing God's mind. It's about changing ours. It's about bringing our hearts, our desires, and our priorities in line with God's plan.

The words "Thy will be done" acknowledge that God's plan isn't necessarily the same as ours. When we are willing to hear what God has to say to us, it changes us. Instead of asking, "Please give me...," we start to ask, "What do you want of me, Lord? Speak, for your servant is listening." Prayer, then, prepares us to be vessels through which God accomplishes his will in the world.

Prayer, the third pillar of Lenten observance, is incredibly important. But prayer is a multifaceted jewel. This week, let's reflect on a few of the many forms of prayer, and put them into practice in our families.

In one of his letters, Saint Paul told the Thessalonians to "pray without ceasing." In other words, pray all the time, all day long. This seems like an awfully big job. But what Paul is trying to tell us is that we should be living our whole lives as if Jesus is walking next to us. We can pray in so many different ways. We can sit by the edge of a creek and be quiet, just enjoying the beautiful world God made. We can say a quick "thank-you" prayer when something makes us happy. We can take a deep breath when we're tempted to do something bad and ask God for help. If we do these things every day, then we are "praying without ceasing."

Reflections

Prayers of praise and thanksgiving

"Praise...lauds God for his own sake and gives him glory... simply because HE IS" (*Catechism of the Catholic Church*, 2639).

Praise is a hard thing to define. So often, wrapped up in daily cares and burdens, we forget about it altogether. But really, praise is the beginning of all prayer. Praise is the part that distracts us from ourselves and puts us face-to-face with God.

When my daughter, who has Down syndrome, was two and a half, she couldn't talk. But she communicated her delight with favorite foods and songs by erupting in a long, loud yell and clapping her hands, showing every one of her teeth. It was essentially a wordless shout of joy. We called it her "yay for the ice cream!" yell. One morning, while I was out running and soaking in the wonder of a beautiful sunrise, I found myself smiling and saying softly, "Yay, God!" That was the first time in my life I really understood the meaning of praise. It's a simple, straightforward emotional response, a way of acknowledging God for his goodness, for the beauty and the wonder of all that he is and all that he gives us.

In a way, praise and thanksgiving are wrapped up together. When we see something worthy of thanking God, it inspires praise. When we praise God, it opens our eyes to the beauty of the world and all we have to be thankful for. The *Catechism of the Catholic Church* says, "The prayer of blessing is man's response to God's gifts" (2626).

God is far bigger than we can possibly comprehend. Prayer begins by acknowledging that there is a higher power in the universe, and we're not it. Once we admit that, it's easier to hear—and to accept—what God is asking of us. Praise is important because it helps us shift our focus from *me* and what *I* want to God and what God wants.

Prayers of petition

Petition is what we most often think of when we speak of prayer. But petition is full of pitfalls. We can get caught up in our concerns and forget that others need prayers. We may try to turn God into a genie who does our bidding instead of the other way around. Or we may think our concerns are too small to bother God with, even though Jesus taught that God numbers every hair on our head. (See Matthew 10:29–30.)

Beginning with praise and thanksgiving helps us approach

prayer with a God-centered mindset. We phrase our prayers with humility, asking for whatever we think we need, yet remaining open to accepting God's answer, whatever it is. *Thy kingdom come. Thy will be done.*

The *Catechism* says, "Christian petition is centered on the desire and *search for the Kingdom to come*....There is a hierarchy in these petitions: we pray first for the Kingdom, then for what is necessary to welcome it and cooperate with its coming" (2632).

Prayer, then, is most of all about what *God* wants for the world. In our petitions, let us focus less on what *we* want and more on facilitating God's will for us.

In the three years my husband and I suffered infertility, we never stopped asking God to bless us with children. But over time, we learned—painfully—that our most important prayer was, *God, please help us to accept your will in our fertility, even though we don't understand it.*

So yes, ask for healing, for kids to sleep through the night, or for good news on a job search. But alongside the requests for tangible benefits, ask for wisdom and patience to bear the uncertainty and for grace to accept God's will if the answer is "no."

Scripture

As Catholics, we are blessed with an incredibly rich tradition of praying through Scripture. Scripture permeates the liturgy; not just the Liturgy of the Word, but the prayers and responses we say and sing throughout the Mass. But the repetition from week to week makes it easy for us all to zone out and not really appreciate the gift of our scriptural worship. And if we adults tune out even though we understand the richness of the gift, how much more do our children miss?

As your children get old enough, help them learn to pay attention to the Mass by explaining the meaning of the prayers and actions. The more they understand, the more likely they are to internalize their faith. During readings and the homily, keep them engaged by "interpreting" as you go. A word of caution, however: this must be done without disrupting the liturgy for those around you. And it is possible to carry explanations too far. Stretch your mind to come up with the most basic explanation that serves the purpose. The car ride home is soon enough to go into greater detail and answer questions.

The *Lectionary* combines readings that draw out a particular theme each day. Over the course of the full *Lectionary* cycle (three years of Sunday readings, two years of daily readings), we encounter a vast amount of the Bible. The Scripture readings are online at http://www.usccb.org/bible/. Try to set aside time to reflect on the daily readings once or twice this week.

Does your family own a good children's Bible? Be sure to read from it regularly to your children. Give them the gift of knowing more than the story of Creation, Noah's Ark, and the birth of Christ. As you read, try to hear the words through the mind of a child. We sometimes take concepts and terms for granted, some of which are key to understanding the point of a story. Stop and ask if your child understands. Ask the child to put it into his or her own words. As with many things in parenthood, you may find that trying to explain it to your child challenges you to dig a little deeper and find answers that enrich your own faith.

The Bible is the inspired Word of God, but it is not meant to be a literal historical record. As children get older, it's important to teach them that some of the stories are not about historical events, but about imparting a lesson. The story of Creation, for instance, really does blend well with scientific theories of evolution. Animal life began in the ocean and the skies and then migrated to land, with humanity as the crowning achievement of Creation. We shouldn't shy away from these subjects. Sooner or later, children are going to be challenged in their beliefs, and the more they know ahead of time, the less likely they are to have their faith shaken.

That said, the lessons have to be done age-appropriately. Overload a child and you're just as likely to undermine their faith as you are to build it up.

Quiet time (contemplative prayer)

After Jesus was baptized, he went into the desert to be alone, away from distraction, and to prepare himself for his public ministry. In the Gospels, Jesus seeks solitude and quiet again and again.

American culture is organized around a constant barrage of stimuli. Texting, Web surfing, music on the radio or iPod—noise and distraction accompany us wherever we go. Does silence make you feel anxious? Yet it is in the quiet that we can hear God, not in the hurricanes of external stimuli.

The *Catholic Encyclopedia* says, "The prayer of quiet is that in which the soul experiences an extraordinary peace and rest, accompanied by delight or pleasure in contemplating God as present." Throughout history, mystics who have practiced contemplative prayer regularly have found that it bears spiritual fruits such as inner peace. These remain with them beyond the prayer itself. And who among us couldn't use more inner peace?

Those who have young children often have trouble finding silence and solitude. But Jesus' example shows that the greater our responsibilities, the more we need that time to re-focus and seek God in the stillness. This week, commit to spending five to ten minutes every day in silence—not talking to God, not reading, but simply being quiet. It may not seem like prayer, but in many ways it is the most powerful prayer of all: simply existing, clearing your mind, not thinking, not talking to God, just listening. After all, God doesn't speak in human words. He speaks in our hearts, and when we are distracted by daily cares and plans, it's hard to hear that still, small voice.

This is not an activity for small children. But if you have older children, encourage them to seek stillness too.

Praying the Stations of the Cross

One of the most poignant prayers of the Church is the Stations of the Cross, which takes on special meaning at this time of year. Observing this devotion as a community helps us focus on Christ's sufferings on our behalf. But it also highlights that Jesus' passion was filled with people who helped him and to whom he ministered: Veronica, the women of Jerusalem, the good thief, and so on. Praying the Stations together helps us remember that we all need to support one another along our Christian journey.

When we pray the Stations of the Cross, we walk beside Jesus through his passion and death. Long ago, people used to make special trips to Jerusalem, where Jesus was crucified, to pray along the road where he carried his cross. They were called "pilgrims." But then Jerusalem was conquered by people who don't believe in Jesus, so people started praying these steps, or stations, in their home parishes.

In the Stations of the Cross, we think about what Jesus did for us, and why he did it. Before Jesus' death and resurrection, the Jewish people used to sacrifice animals on a special altar. The lamb was called the "paschal lamb," and it was killed to take away their sins. But they had to do it over and over again. Jesus offered himself as the paschal lamb. He died to take away all our sins, for everyone in the world, for all the rest of time. The Eucharist we share at Mass is our most important way of remembering Jesus' sacrifice, but during Lent, we use the Stations to help make it all a little more real.

Activities

Attend Stations of the Cross as a family. Check with your parish for times. Parochial schools often pray the Stations as well, and the reflections and prayers will almost always be aimed at young people.

Set up family prayer time. This can take place before the family members leave the dinner table or it can take place at bedtime, with all the children kneeling around a bed. Whatever works to bring your family together is fine. Read the daily Scriptures (or a portion of them); take time to incorporate silence, praise, and thanksgiving as well as petitions. Encourage each family member to share whatever is on his or her mind so that the family can rejoice and petition together.

Your Easter Tree

Make prayer flowers. Using the templates in Appendix B, make prayer flowers, using one color or style for praise and thanks and a different color for petitions. This is an ongoing project. From now until Easter, any time you hear of someone who needs prayers, add his or her name to your tree. Encourage your children to make a leaf anytime they see something they want to praise God for. Remind them often to look for opportunities to praise God in the ordinary moments of life.

For the Children

Prayers of praise: What do you think of when you hear the word *praise*? Praise really isn't about words we speak. It's about seeing things all around us that God made or that God gave us and being happy just because they're there. It's like seeing a beautiful rainbow and saying, "Yay, God! What a pretty rainbow! Yay, God! I really love my mom (or dad)!"

What is something that makes you happy? Write or draw a picture of it on a leaf and put it on your Easter Tree.

Prayers of petition: God asks us to pray for whatever we need, but also for other people. When your grandma is sick or your best friend's dad loses his job, you can pray for them too. Think of something you want to ask God to give you. Then think of someone who needs prayers, and write that person's name or draw a picture of the person on a leaf and put it on your Easter Tree.

Stations of the Cross "pilgrimage." After your family trip to the Stations of the Cross (see Week One Activities on page 39) or after another special trip to a local parish or outdoor Stations of the Cross, ask your children to reflect on the experience. Have each child draw a picture of the station that means the most to them on an Easter Tree leaf. Have them explain why they are drawn to this particular station.

SECOND WEEK

Baptism and the RCIA

On Easter Sunday, regardless of whether a baptism takes place, the entire community renews its baptismal promises. There's a reason for this. We're returning to our roots.

In the early years of the Church, becoming a Christian took a long time. Adults who wanted to convert went through a process of testing and instruction that often lasted several years. Becoming a Christian was a huge, life-altering decision—much more than it is today. In the pagan world, following Christ often meant grisly execution. People had to totally change their way of life. The Church wanted to make sure its new members would "stick," and the best way to do that was to support them through an extended process. This process ended in an intensive period of fasting and ritual preparation just before Easter, which was the only time of year people were baptized.

After Christianity became legal in the fourth century, things relaxed, and eventually the catechumenate disappeared altogether. But the fast in preparation for Easter had taken firm hold among the faithful. Thus, Lent was born.

After the Second Vatican Council, the Church returned to its ancient practice by bringing people into the Church through a process we know as the Rite of Christian Initiation for Adults, or RCIA. Now, adults who wish to join the Church go through a yearlong process of study and preparation. These "Inquirers" include both "catechumens" (those who have never been baptized) and "candidates" (those who are already Christians but want to become Catholics).

A few months before Easter, the parish community celebrates the Rite of Acceptance, after which the Inquirers begin attending the Liturgy of the Word with the parish on Sundays.

But it is during Lent that the process really intensifies. With the Rite of Sending and the Rite of Election at the beginning of Lent, the Elect, as they are now called, enter the last phase of preparation for receiving the sacraments of initiation at the Easter Vigil.

During Lent, the community prepares alongside them—only in our case, we are preparing to renew our baptismal vows, not baptism itself. On the third, fourth, and fifth Sundays of Lent, we participate in "Scrutinies," which replace the prayers of the faithful and call us to examine the influences that keep us from following Christ wholeheartedly. The Easter Vigil, with its long procession of baptisms, confirmations, and first Communions, is a celebration intended for the whole community.

As members of the community, it is our responsibility to support those in the RCIA through the process. But shadowing them through their journey, especially during Lent, gives us a chance to experience our own story of conversion again and again.

For the Children

On Easter Sunday, we don't say the usual Creed that starts, "I believe in one God, the Father almighty...." Instead, the priest asks us the questions that are part of baptizing a baby. This is called the "renewal of our baptismal promises," and there's a lot more to them than what's in the Creed. This is the reason we fast and pray during Lent. We're getting ourselves ready to promise Jesus all over again that we'll follow him.

From now until Easter, we'll see a lot of extra stuff going on at Sunday Mass. The people who are getting ready to join the Church go through something called "RCIA." But it's not just for them, it's for us too—our job is to pray for them and with them and to show them what it means to be Catholic by the way we live our lives. We walk the journey with them, and that makes it all the more special when we renew our baptismal promises at Easter.

Reflections

Sacraments are an outward sign of an inner mystical reality—a place where God and the physical world touch. Because we are physical beings, we need physical signs to help us internalize that which is invisible. As the basic sacrament of Christianity, baptism is particularly rich in these physical symbols. Let's explore some of them more deeply this week.

Water

Water is everywhere in our world—covering perhaps 70 percent of the surface of the Earth and making up two thirds of our bodies. It comes out of the tap at the turn of a knob; we use it, waste it, every day without ever stopping to think that without it, life could not exist.

The centrality of water to human life makes it a natural symbol of Christian life too. In the blessing over the water, prayed at every Catholic baptism, we trace the many ways in which water changed the course of life for God's people:

- The Holy Spirit breathing upon the waters at Creation
- The Great Flood wiping out sin in the world
- The people of Israel escaping from bondage through the Red Sea
- Jesus being baptized in the Jordan River
- Water and blood flowing from Jesus' side upon the Cross
- Jesus' sending out his disciples to baptize all nations

In baptism, water washes away our sins and frees us from the bondage of sin. In baptism, we die to sin and are reborn in the life of God.

For the Children

Do you remember how the Book of Genesis starts? In the beginning, there was nothing—just the wind sweeping over the waters. God took that water and made it into something life-giving. That's the same way we look at water in baptism.

Water was really important to people in biblical times. They lived in a desert and water was hard to find, so the Bible often compares God's love to flowing waters and green trees that grow beside water. When Moses led the Israelites out of slavery in Egypt, he led them through the Red Sea—waters that parted to let them through and then covered and killed the Egyptians. When Jesus was baptized, he was dunked under the water, the same way grownups are baptized in our church at the Easter Vigil.

We all know water is really important: it makes things grow, we need it to drink, and it cleanses us. But it's also dangerous. We can drown in water if we're not careful. And that is something we also remember by using water in baptism. The water shows us our sinful self is dying.

Light

In the beginning, all was darkness. The first words God spoke into the void were, "Let there be light." As humans, we seem to have a natural aversion to darkness. We don't feel safe in it. Children fill it with imaginary monsters, and adults fill it with axe-wielding villains. Light and darkness are a pair of opposites that have found a home in every age of literature, representing good and evil. Yet the Gospel of John pounds the lesson home again and again: the real darkness is sin, and Christ is the Light of the world.

When we light a baptismal candle, we pledge to walk as a child of the Light. As parents and godparents, our job is to keep the flame of faith burning for our children—and for ourselves, so that like the wise virgins in Jesus' parable (Matthew 25), we are always ready to greet Christ when he comes again.

Tonight, pull out your children's baptismal candles and burn them for a few minutes at dinner or during family prayer time. You can't burn them for too long, or in a few years they'll be gone, but letting children see their candle lit will make the symbol more real to them.

For the Children

Before you were born, you lived in the darkness of your mother's womb. When you were born, you found a whole new world full of light and beautiful things. In baptism, Jesus invites us to be born again, only this time the dark place where we live is the darkness of sin, and we're being called into "his wonderful light," as we hear during a baptism. Each of us received a special candle when we were baptized. It was lit from the Easter candle, which symbolizes Jesus, who is the Light of the world.

White garment

Like light and water, the color white evokes purity and cleanliness. Because it shows stains so easily, there is no better image to hold up for us as Christians. The white garment shows that our souls are *clothed with Christ*. The garment is a visible sign of Christ's presence within us and a reminder to guard the purity of our newly washed souls so that we may bring them unstained into heaven when we die.

Pull out the white garments your children wore for their baptism and let them touch the fabric.

For the Children

White clothes are really hard to keep clean. Have you ever noticed that? We tend to save white clothes for very special occasions, like weddings and baptisms. That's because they show dirt so easily, and those are the times when we want to show that we are pure. To be pure means that our souls—the part of us that is made in God's image—are clean, free from sin.

Activities

Have a baptism party. Pull out the baptismal candles, have everyone wear white, and celebrate with a special cake that says, "I am a child of God."

Take a tour of a baptismal font at your local church. Notice how it is decorated. Are there plants that need water to survive? Take along a small container for each child, and let each collect some holy water to bring home. If you have holy water fonts lying around in a closet or a drawer somewhere, this is the time to pull them out and put them on the wall. That way, family members can remind themselves of their baptismal commitment often.

Your Easter Tree

Call the parish office and ask the director of religious education for the name of a candidate or catechumen to adopt in prayer. Put his or her name on a flower and mount it on your tree. It would also be nice to invite the person over for dinner at least once during Lent.

On an Easter Tree leaf, have your children draw something that needs water to survive.

Carol Basi's Fish Soup

The first time my soon-to-be mother-in-law offered me this soup, I had my reservations. But it's a delicious soup. My in-laws' Italian family serve this on Christmas Eve, but I have come to appreciate it as a light meal for Lent as well.

Note: all quantities are approximate.

> 3 T. olive oil
> 3-5 cloves garlic, minced
> 1 medium onion, chopped
> 2–3 stalks of celery, including inside leaves, chopped
> 28-oz. can diced tomatoes
> ⅓ can water
> 1 lb. Seafood (shrimp, clams, cod, haddock,
> scallops, and so forth)
> Salt and pepper to taste

Sauté onion and garlic in olive oil. Add remaining ingredients and simmer for 15 minutes.

Approximately 15–20 minutes before serving, add the seafood. The more expensive fish make a tastier soup with better texture, but you can also use whatever is on sale.

Serve with garlic bread and salad or vegetable.

THIRD WEEK

Have you ever wondered why Adam and Eve ate fruit from the tree of knowledge? After all, they had everything they needed and a God who had given it to them. Why should they have been tempted at all? The standard answer is human pride: they thought if they ate it, they would become like God—equals with the Maker of the universe.

Of course, it didn't quite turn out that way. All they managed to do was cut themselves off from the one Being in the whole universe who made them feel complete. Ever since, human beings have been looking for that Being, seeking something to fill the emptiness inside us. Sometimes, we find God in the people and places of our daily lives. But a lot of times, we end up trying to replace God with something else—something of Earth. And that's where we get into trouble.

When you think about it, it's a good thing we have this season every year. In our fast-paced world, we tend to get distracted by clutter. The very things that make Lent so trying—fasting and self-denial—are exactly what make it so powerful. There's nothing like fasting and self-denial to put everything in perspective. Lent is our chance to wash out the white baptismal garment after it gets grimy from use.

During Lent more than any other time of the year, we get to focus on restoring what has been broken: our connection with God. It's just human nature—if we don't spend quality time with the ones we love, we start bickering with them instead. It's the same way with God. Every so often, we need a chance to retreat, to go into the desert and get reacquainted with God.

We tend to think of repentance as a negative—a spotlight on how bad we are. Then, not content with feeling guilty about our sins, we set out to punish ourselves with all kinds of penance. (No wonder the sacrament of reconciliation has fallen off in popularity!) Instead, perhaps we should look at repentance in light of its origin.

The Hebrew word *shuwb* means "to turn back, to turn aside." It's a subtle difference perhaps, but one that infuses the concept with hope instead of dreary misery. What if we see repentance as an opportunity to set aside bad spiritual habits and attitudes—gossip, self-absorption, greed—and replace them with practices that enrich life and bring us closer to the God we long for? If we really take time to think about it, Lent is an amazing gift. Just when our resolve to make this year different from the last disappears into the dreary winter of reality, Lent arrives, offering us a fresh start.

Don't get me wrong—we are all sinners, and we need to acknowledge that to feel contrition. Indeed, without that element, it's unlikely we'll make any meaningful change at all. But as Catholics, we're doubly blessed with the sacrament of reconciliation. Not only can we explore new beginnings on our own, but we have a sacrament to make it official. And it's a sacrament that is not dependent on a season.

Reflection

Fess up! The sacrament of reconciliation

It takes a strong soul not to feel nervous about going to confession. There's just something so vulnerable about it. You come before God's representative and stammer your way through all the bad things you've done—things you'd rather pretend never happened—hoping you don't miss anything important.

And yet if we come to the sacrament of reconciliation with open hearts, it can be such a grace-filled experience. Like a stone thrown into a still pond, every sin we commit sends ripples into our families, our workplaces, and our parishes. Pride, selfishness, gossip, judgment, and so on tear the fabric of our community and pave the way to hard feelings and damaged relationships. Reconciliation gives us the chance to heal the rifts in our relationships—if we're courageous enough to fess up.

Coming face-to-face with our own weaknesses can be painful, and it's natural for us to be filled with sorrow. But naming our sins aloud to the priest opens the door to something truly miraculous: God wipes the slate clean. Gone. Done. No three strikes, no points on your record; it's a brand-new day.

For the Children

Have you ever done something bad but nobody knew about it? It just sits there inside you, squeezing on your heart until you can't enjoy anything. What happens after you tell your mom or your dad what you did? Don't you feel better, even if you get in trouble?

This is why we have the sacrament of reconciliation. We get to tell God, through his servant the priest, what we have done wrong and receive forgiveness. But even if you're not old enough to go to confession, you can still tell God you're sorry for your sins. When you know you have done something wrong, ask God to forgive you, and then try to make things better. If you took something from your brother, give it back and tell him you're sorry. If you called a classmate a name, apologize to her. Sometimes it's really hard to do this, but you will always feel better afterward, because you'll know you've done whatever you can to make things right.

Activities

Spring is near. Why not spend some time this week putting your home and your heart in order? Here are some suggestions:

Charitable challenge. Challenge every member of your family to come up with a specific number of things to give to charity. You can choose one item or ten, clothes or books or toys—just make sure that as you clean the toy chests and the closets, the family is also thinking about those in need and praying for those who will benefit from your family's bounty.

Nix the negativity. Negativity, complaining, and gossip—almost all of us are guilty of these bad habits, and we learn them by example. This week challenge your family members—and more importantly, yourself—to keep negative words to themselves.

Seek reconciliation as a family. This week, go to confession as a family. Prepare ahead of time by making an examination of conscience together, even if your children are too young to receive the sacrament.

Your Easter Tree

Spending time in the desert. Have your children write down or draw a picture of what they have learned about God so far this Lent on an Easter Tree leaf.

For the Children

Have you ever seen a desert? There's not a whole lot there. People don't spend much time in the desert because there's not much to eat or drink and not much to do. It's easier to hear God in the desert because a bunch of other things are not trying to get our attention.

Lent is kind of like a desert: when we give things up, we take away some of what is distracting us from God. So then we have more attention to focus on him. Have you learned anything about God so far this Lent? Let's decorate our Easter Tree with these lessons.

Recipe

Pasta Primavera

The vegetables can be tweaked to reflect the season or the contents of your refrigerator.

3-5 T. olive oil and/or butter

3-5 cloves garlic, minced

1 onion, sliced

2 zucchini, sliced into medallions

1 yellow squash, sliced into medallions

1 bunch asparagus, cut into bite-sized pieces

1 head broccoli, cut into bite-sized pieces

8 oz. mushrooms, sliced

1 can chicken broth or cream of mushroom soup

1 lb. fettuccine or penne

Cook pasta according to package directions.

Meanwhile, heat olive oil and/or butter in a large skillet over medium heat. Sauté garlic briefly (the garlic should not brown); add onion, broccoli, zucchini, squash, and asparagus. Cook, stirring often, for 7–10 minutes. Turn heat to high and add mushrooms, along with more oil or butter if necessary (mushrooms soak up the liquid); cook another 3–5 minutes. Add soup or broth (broth is a lighter flavor; mushroom soup adds body and richness). Continue to stir and cook for 3–4 minutes. When the mixture is well incorporated, drain the pasta and mix with vegetables in a large serving bowl. Serve with freshly grated Parmesan.

Note: Parmesan cheese is available at most grocery stores in a triangular block. Cheese should melt on hot food.

LENT

FOURTH WEEK

Renewal

Spring is coming in the Northern Hemisphere. Perhaps it's already peeking through the ground in the form of crocuses or daffodils, even tulips, depending on where you live. The air is warming, the first birds are returning from their winter homes, and in the next few weeks, the world will undergo a miraculous transformation. What better time to journey through Lent—to let our hearts undergo the same transformation?

We begin this season mired in the depths of dreary winter, with trees and flowers dead or dormant. With the holidays past, we trudge through a bleak landscape, starved for fresh air, sunlight, and color—much like our souls in the grip of sin. The "desert" of the winter landscape acts as a mirror, reflecting all the bad habits we've allowed to pile up in the past year and how far we have wandered from God.

But Lent takes the bitterness of alienation and sin and splashes color, vibrancy, and hope all over it. At no other time of the year do we see so clearly that death is not an end, but the gateway into life. When things seem the most hopeless, it's easier to let go and get out of God's way. When we do, the Spirit pours in and makes us new.

Reflection

Journeying

We tend to think of Lent as a time to hang out in the "desert," which we interpret as lifeless, full of misery, temptation, and trial. But Lent is a journey, not a destination: a journey from death to life.

For the Children

The word *Lent* comes from an Old English word, *Lencten*. Can you hear how it sounds like "lengthen"? This was the word for spring—a word that meant the days were growing longer. We are halfway through our journey. Are the days getting longer as we get closer to the full glory of Easter and Jesus' resurrection?

How do you feel after all the work you have done? Can you feel God in a different way than you did before Lent began?

Activities

Start some seeds. You will need small pots, packets of seeds, potting soil, and water.

Unless a grain of wheat falls to the ground and dies, it remains just a grain of wheat; but if it dies, it produces much fruit.

JOHN 12:24

Read the above Scripture to your children, and then give them an opportunity to see springtime renewal in action. Let them start flower seeds or vegetables for a summer garden. Do your homework. Find out how much water your chosen plant needs, how often, and how much sunshine. Nothing can undermine the lesson more quickly than a plant that dies due to overwatering!

Go on a picnic and nature walk. Pack a lunch and go out to a park where the family can enjoy spring. In praying over your meal, be sure to thank God for the specific signs of spring that you can see, hear, or smell around you.

Clean up creation. Last week, we did some spring cleaning for our souls. This week, give God's gift of creation a spring cleaning by picking up litter from a nearby creek, street, or park.

Bring spring to those who need it most. Nursing homes, food pantries, and others who care for society's most vulnerable receive lots of donations and attention around Christmas, but the need is just as great at other times of the year. Bring God's creation to those who can't get outdoors: pick flowers, make homemade cards with spring scenes, or bake flower-shaped cookies and take them to a nursing home or to a shut-in neighbor.

Your Easter Tree

Each day this week, look for some new sign of spring and bring it to your Easter Tree.

For the Children

Every spring, God takes everything that was dead and brings it back to life—just like Jesus. Baby animals are born, grass turns green, and flowers bloom. Spring helps us understand what it means to rise from the dead. Let's look for all the signs that spring is coming and make leaves of them to hang on the Easter Tree.

Don't forget your praise, thanksgiving, and petition leaves and flowers! Are you still adding new ones?

Italian Red Sauce

Straight from the kitchen of my husband's grandmother, who came to America as a young girl, this recipe is surprisingly simple and easy to make.

⅓ cup olive oil

3 cloves garlic

28-oz. can tomatoes (diced or crushed is easiest)

14-oz. can tomato sauce

6-oz. can tomato paste

Salt, if desired

1 T. oregano

1 T. parsley

1 T. basil

In a medium pot, simmer garlic in olive oil until fragrant, but do not let it brown. Add the rest of the ingredients.

Simmer on very low heat for two hours, stirring frequently. Serve over pasta.

Note: Cook Italian sausage in a skillet and add to sauce along with the grease for a meaty version of this recipe for non-Friday use.

LENT

FIFTH WEEK

Passover

The time is drawing near. As we get closer and closer to the celebration that anchors our faith, let's pause to reflect on the context of Holy Week.

In the Book of Genesis, Israel and his family went to Egypt to escape a famine. There, they found their brother Joseph, who had become a person of influence in Pharaoh's court. The reunited family settled in Egypt and prospered; the family grew. And grew. Suddenly Pharaoh wasn't so sure he liked having all these Jews hanging around, being so prosperous. So he started taxing them; he put them to work building pyramids. And pretty soon the people of Israel had fallen from prosperity into slavery.

Enter Moses. God sent Moses to Pharaoh with a simple message: "Let my people go" (Exodus 9:1). But no matter what plagues and pestilences God sent on the Egyptians, Pharaoh remained unmoved. So God upped the ante. "I'm going to send the Angel of Death through," he said, "and every firstborn child is going to die—cattle, goats, sheep, people."

The Israelites got their instructions loud and clear too: *This is it, folks, this is the night of your deliverance. Pack up and be ready to go.* God told them to sacrifice a lamb—the paschal lamb—and smear its blood on the doorposts so the angel of the Lord would pass over and leave all inhabitants unharmed. They ate the lamb along with unleavened bread.

We all know what happened next. With his firstborn son ripped from him, Pharaoh finally capitulated, and the Israelites crossed the sea to freedom on dry ground while Pharaoh's chariots were lost in the deluge. God's people were free.

This is the feast Jesus was celebrating the night before he died. At that meal of roasted lamb and unleavened bread, the themes of captivity and freedom, sacrifice and salvation, surely were foremost in every mind. No one who heard Jesus fire these words out into history could doubt what he meant: "This is my body, given up for you." Especially not after what happened the next day when he went like a lamb to the slaughter.

But unlike the yearly ritual slaughters these faithful Jewish people had observed for millennia, the sacrifice of the paschal lamb doesn't have to be offered again and again. Jesus willingly took on the sins of the world and poured out his lifeblood for us.

Activities

Easter Story Eggs and the Easter Tree

This week, we will start our Easter Story Eggs, which we will continue to use through Holy Week to Easter. This popular activity for children involves a dozen plastic eggs, each of which contains a symbol of something connected to the passion, death, and resurrection of Christ. The following list contains fourteen suggestions. Choose the twelve that seem most appropriate to you.

To prepare the eggs, collect the symbols, place one inside each plastic egg, and nest them in an egg carton before the week begins. If you have older children, this would be a great activity for them to prepare for their younger siblings.

On Monday through Saturday of this week, let a child open an egg. Read the italicized explanations to your children and/or the Scripture passages provided. Better yet, ask them if they know what each item symbolizes. Then have the children make a new leaf for the Easter Tree with a picture of the item. If you are using a three-dimensional tree, you can hang the symbol itself.

- **A picture of a donkey, a palm leaf, or a piece of last year's Palm Sunday palms**
- **Scripture reference: Luke 19:28–38**

Just a few short days before Jesus' crucifixion, he rode into Jerusalem on a donkey, and people threw down palm branches before him. He'd become so famous that they treated him like a king. We remember this on Palm Sunday.

- **A miniature cup (from a doll-house set), a small medicine cup (the ones they include with children's medicines), a water-bottle lid, or a small piece of bread**
- **Scripture reference: Matthew 26:26–29**

While Jesus was in Jerusalem, he celebrated Passover with his Apostles. Passover is the most important feast in the Jewish faith because it reminds Jews of the night God delivered them from slavery in Egypt. The Passover meal is unleavened bread (meaning it has no yeast) and a special lamb sacrificed to God. That night in Jerusalem, Jesus took that simple meal and changed its meaning forever. Now he is the Lamb sacrificed to God; the bread is his Body and the wine is his Blood.

- **A silk or plastic flower**
- **Scripture reference: Matthew 26:36–46**

After the Last Supper, Jesus went out to the Garden of Gethsemane to pray. He knew what was going to happen to him and he was scared, so he prayed. But his friends couldn't stay awake with him.

- **Three dimes**
- **Scripture reference: Matthew 26:47–50**

Judas was one of Jesus' closest followers, and yet he went to the chief priests, who were afraid of Jesus, and offered to betray him. They gave Judas thirty pieces of silver. He took the chief priests to the garden where Jesus was praying and kissed him. Then they arrested Jesus. This was the beginning of his passion.

- **A piece of leather, a small piece of rope, or a thick string**
- **Scripture reference: Mark 15:1–15**

The Jews sent Jesus to Pontius Pilate, who had him scourged. This means he was whipped with a leather strip until he bled.

- **A thorn or thorny branch (such as a dead branch from a rosebush)**
- **Scripture reference: Mark 15:16–20**

Pontius Pilate had his soldiers make a crown or a cap of thorns and place it on Jesus' head to make fun of him since he was called the "King of the Jews."

- **A small cross**
- **Scripture reference: Matthew 27:32**

Jesus had to carry his cross from Pilate's court to the hill of Golgotha. He fell three times along the way, and the soldiers grabbed a man named Simon of Cyrene out of the crowd to help him.

- **A nail**
- **Scripture reference: John 19:16b–18**

Jesus carried his cross to the hill of Golgotha, and they nailed him to it and left him there to die.

- **Slip of paper reading "Jesus the Nazorean, the King of the Jews" (or INRI)**
- **Scripture reference: John 19:19**

This is what Pontius Pilate put on the cross so that everyone would know why he was being killed. But it was because he took all our sins away that we now know Jesus as our king too.

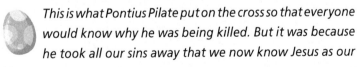

- **Dice or a small square of fabric**
- **Scripture reference: John 19:23–24**

While Jesus was on the cross, the Roman soldiers played games to decide who would get his clothes after he died.

- **Sponge**
- **Scripture reference: John 19:28–30**

Jesus asked for a drink, and they couldn't reach him because he was up so high. So they took a sponge, stuck it on a stick, and put it up to his mouth so he could drink.

- **A rock**
- **Scripture reference: Luke 23:50–53**

After Jesus died, a holy man named Joseph of Arimathea came and took Jesus' body to bury it in a cave. They covered the cave with a rock that was too heavy for anyone to move alone.

- **Spices, such as a few whole cloves**
- **Scripture reference: Luke 23:54–56**

On Easter Sunday morning, some women who loved Jesus came to the tomb to anoint his body with spices. They hadn't had time to do it the day he died, because the holy day was coming and they weren't allowed to work after sundown. So they came first thing in the morning the day after Passover.

- **Leave one egg empty**
- **Scripture reference: Matthew 28:6**

 When the women came to anoint Jesus' body, they found the stone had been rolled away, and the tomb was empty. Jesus had risen from the dead!

LENT

HOLY WEEK

Christ's Passion and Death

Technically speaking, Lent ends after Wednesday of Holy Week. What follows are three days known as Triduum. But it's three days counted in a funny way. In ancient Jewish tradition, sundown was not only the end of one day but the beginning of the next. After all, they didn't have clocks to tell them it was midnight, so they used the cycles of nature to give structure to their days. Triduum, too, follows this pattern. Triduum encompasses three twenty-four–hour periods over four calendar days: Holy Thursday, Good Friday, Holy Saturday, and Easter Sunday. Although the Church celebrates four separate services during these days, Thursday, Friday, and Saturday are considered a single liturgy.

Although these are long services, within them we find all the richness Catholicism has to offer. The events we remember on these three days are the origin of all Christianity. Make it a family tradition to attend as much as you can of the Triduum liturgy.

What sets us apart from many other Christian denominations is the Church's recognition that we are people of the body as well as the spirit. Faith cannot be fed by words alone; it must be experienced and lived out using our bodies. Every sacrament contains a tangible, physical symbol, because although we serve God who is beyond sense, we serve him using our bodies, and our bodies must be part of the act of worship. At no other time of the year is this made clearer than during Triduum.

Reflections

Holy Thursday:
celebration of the Lord's Supper

Holy Thursday commemorates the institution of the priesthood and the Eucharist. What exactly does that mean? It means tonight is our memorial of the night it all began: the night Jesus spoke the words, "Do this in memory of me" to his Apostles, making them the first priests, sharing the first celebration of the Eucharist.

The first thing we notice on Thursday night is the color. The earthy purple of Lent gives way to white, the color of rejoicing, of high feast days. Generally, the music is more exuberant than the preceding weeks. We sing the Gloria, and following the homily, the priest(s) and deacon(s) imitate Jesus' washing the feet of his Apostles. Some parishes take this more literally than others, choosing twelve men to represent the twelve Apostles. Others treat it as an invitation to the whole assembly, and one person washes the feet of the next. Still others choose something in the middle. However it plays out, this is a moment when children pay attention. They know this story; to see it played out before their very eyes is very powerful.

At the offertory, the priest receives the oils that will be used in parish life for the next year: the oil of the catechumens, the oil of the sick, and the oil of chrism. Following Communion, the exuberance of the early part of the celebration tones down as we look ahead to the memorial of the passion. The altar is stripped bare, the candles removed, and the Blessed Sacrament, accompanied by the ancient chant "Pange Lingua," travels in procession to a place of reverence, where people are invited to stay and pray for a portion of the night.

For the Children

When we go to church on Holy Thursday night, we are starting one long liturgy, or celebration, that lasts three days. Tonight is the celebration of the Lord's Supper. The priests and deacons will wash the feet of some of our parishioners, just like Jesus washed his disciples' feet. During the offertory, we will bring up the oils our priests and deacons use to baptize children and anoint the sick. After Communion, Father will carry the Eucharist in procession to a place where people will stay and pray with Jesus, just as he asked his friends to do in the Garden of Gethsemane before he was arrested.

Good Friday: the Passion

Good Friday is the only day of the year when Mass is not allowed to be celebrated. Instead, we have a Communion service that begins in silence, with the priest, deacon, and servers lying prostrate on the floor. Since this is a continuation of the liturgy begun on Holy Thursday, we skip the opening rites and go straight to the readings. Tonight we hear Isaiah's description of the suffering servant as well as Saint John's Passion. The service also includes veneration of the cross—another opportunity for children to make a tactile connection to the events we commemorate. Perhaps the longest part of the evening comes in the lengthy prayers of the faithful, which are chanted by the deacon and priest in conversation. In the middle of each prayer, we kneel in silence. The service then moves quickly through the setting of the altar and Communion. Again, the night ends in silence.

For the Children

Good Friday is the only day of the year on which Mass is not celebrated. We receive Communion, but only because the priest consecrated it the night before. Tonight we hear the prophet Isaiah talk about the "suffering servant," and we read the Passion—the story of Jesus' death. After the homily, we venerate the cross. This means we come up to touch or to kiss it and to say a quick prayer.

Holy Saturday: the Easter Vigil

What to say about Easter Vigil? It's long. It's late. Yes, of course it is. But here, in this one spectacular evening, we celebrate the core of everything we are as Christians.

Light The Vigil begins with the lighting of the Easter fire and the Easter candle, which in many parishes then spreads from person to person as the candle enters the church. When the candle reaches the front, the deacon sings the Exsultet, a breathtaking prayer that reminds us of God's love for his people and all the ways light figures into it.

Word The Easter Vigil contains nine readings, most of which have responsorial psalms. It's like a one-hour tour of salvation history. Many parishes cut the list to shorten the liturgy, but the full list includes Creation, Abraham and Isaac, the Exodus, and several prophecies showing how the covenant between God and his people was made, broken, and renewed. From Paul's Letter to the Romans we hear about Christ's rising from the dead. The Gospel, of course, is the resurrection story.

Initiation The catechumens (those who have not been baptized) and candidates (those who were baptized into other Christian denominations) are baptized and confirmed.

Table After the rites of initiation, Mass proceeds as usual, if you can call the miracle of Christ among us "usual." Celebrating the Eucharist with the "neophytes" (new Catholics) can be a deeply moving experience for cradle Catholics, who tend to take the sacrament for granted.

For the Children

Tonight is the Easter Vigil, which completes our celebration of Holy Week. It begins with the lighting of the Easter candle. Instead of three readings, we have nine. These readings take a while, but they help us to see how God's plan stays the same, no matter what we do, and how he can always make things right, no matter how bad they seem. Tonight, the people we've been praying for in the RCIA finally get to be baptized and confirmed and receive the Eucharist.

Activities

Our focus this week is on the liturgies we have spent the last six weeks preparing for. So keep the extra liturgical activities simple.

Perhaps it is not possible to expect children to sit through church three days in a row. If your children are too young to make family attendance at Triduum a reality, bring the celebration home.

Holy Thursday

Set up a special place in your home where the family can gather for the evening ritual. Put a small table by the Easter Tree, and drape it with a white cloth. Decorate it with a loaf of bread, a cup of wine (or juice), a bowl of water, and a few white hand towels. Read the story of the Last Supper from a children's Bible, and then reenact the washing of the feet in whatever way is most appropriate for your family. Pass the bread and cup around, just as Jesus did, and finish with family prayer time.

Today is Holy Thursday. On this day we remember the Last Supper, which Jesus celebrated with his Apostles the night before he died. You'll recognize the words from the story we read tonight, because the priest says them at every Mass. This was the night when Jesus gave us the Eucharist. It's also the night when Jesus showed everyone that we have to serve one another. He did this by washing his disciples' feet. Tonight we'll do that too.

Good Friday

If schedules prevent you from attending a Good Friday service, try to make a special trip to church to pray. Tonight, drape the table in red and set a cross or crucifix on it. Read the Passion from a children's Bible, venerate the cross, perhaps passing it from person to person, and finish with family prayer time.

Holy Saturday

In the evening, drape the table in white and decorate it with a cross and flowers, and perhaps with some Resurrection Rolls (see recipe on page 83). Even after your children are old enough to attend Triduum liturgies with the parish family, decorating the table for each day of the weekend can be a great way to keep the family focused on Christ.

Tell the story of salvation history to your children in your own words, or in words such as this:

When God created the world, he meant for us to live with him forever, being happy and doing what is right. But Adam and Eve sinned, and so do we. But still, God loved us so much that he wanted us to be a family. So he promised Abraham that he would have as many children and grandchildren as there are stars in the sky.

God kept his promise. Abraham's children became a great nation—the nation of Israel. But the Israelites also sinned, and eventually they ended up being slaves of Pharaoh, the king of Egypt. God spoke to a man named Moses and told him to lead the Israelites out of slavery. God parted the waters of the Red Sea to help them escape

Pharaoh. God made a new covenant with the Israelites, promising to love them forever.

But even after all this, the Israelites turned their back on God again and again. Sometimes God would get angry and would punish them. But then they would say they were sorry, and God would forgive them.

Finally God sent Jesus to make a new covenant with us. Jesus is God's Son—fully divine, just like God—but also fully human, just like us. Jesus became the bridge between God and people on Earth. When Jesus offered his life on the cross, he did it to make peace for all of our sins. And when he rose from the dead, he took away the power of sin and death. Now, even though someday our bodies will die, our souls will live forever with God and Jesus in heaven.

Resurrection rolls

At its most basic, a Resurrection Roll is a large marshmallow sealed inside a roll. The marshmallow will melt during baking, leaving a hole in the middle. This symbolizes the empty tomb. If you want, you can dress them up by dipping the marshmallows in melted butter and rolling them in cinnamon sugar, which represent the spices and oils used to anoint Jesus' body. (See next page for recipe.)

Easter Story Eggs

Refer to the list on pages 68–72 to continue opening Easter Story Eggs this week with your children.

Recipe

Sweet-Potato Resurrection Rolls

Although I give directions here for using a stand mixer, it will work great in a bread machine or a food processor too.

2 medium sweet potatoes, cooked, peeled, and mashed
4 T. firmly-packed brown sugar
4 T. butter, room temperature
1 tsp. salt
½ to 1 tsp. cinnamon, to taste
4 cups flour
2 tsp. (one packet) active dry yeast
1 bag large marshmallows
Cinnamon sugar
Melted butter
Milk, for brushing on top

Place sweet potatoes in a pan and cover with water. Bring to a boil, reduce heat, and simmer for 15 minutes or until a fork pierces the thickest part easily. Drain, and reserve ¼ cup water. Peel and mash.

Mix 1 cup sweet-potato puree, brown sugar, butter, salt, and cinnamon in a large mixing bowl until combined. Add flour and yeast and mix at low speed. Using a dough hook, knead at medium speed for 5–7 minutes (or turn onto floured surface and knead by hand). Texture should be smooth and elastic. Knead in more flour if dough is sticky.

Transfer to a greased bowl and cover with plastic. Let rise for 1½–2 hours, until double in volume.

Roll dough into thin 5-inch circles. Then prepare the marshmallows. Melt butter; dip marshmallows in the butter, then roll in cinnamon sugar. Place a marshmallow at the center of each circle. Fold the circle up and pinch together at the top. Be sure it seals, or the marshmallow will ooze out during baking. Place on a greased baking sheet and brush with milk. Bake at 350 for 15 minutes.

Note 1: To make cloverleaf rolls without the marshmallow, grease a muffin tin, then roll 3 small balls and arrange them in a triangle in each cup. Let them rise for 30–40 minutes, then bake at 375 for 20–25 minutes.

Note 2: You can also use store-bought crescent-roll dough to wrap the marshmallows. This may be easier, especially for families that don't do a lot of from-scratch baking.

He Is Risen, Alleluia!

Our Lenten journey has ended, but our wanderings are far from over. Today, among the crowds of people and the heady odor of lilies and incense, try to imagine what it must have been like for the Apostles. In the past few days, they had experienced the worst moments of their lives. Now, at the empty tomb, on the road to Emmaus, in locked rooms and on a mountaintop, they finally began to understand: the heaviest cross, the most hopeless death, means nothing beside God's promise.

Life may be encapsulated by moments, both good and bad. But it is what we do in transit that gives those moments meaning. On this first day of Easter—a season that most years will stretch beyond the end of school and into summer—let us remember the lessons learned in the desert and carry them with us as we journey onward.

He Is Risen, Alleluia!

Celebrating Feast Days During Lent

In this book, I have offered suggestions for each week of Lent. But as Catholics, we also interrupt our Lenten fasting to celebrate saints and various events in the life of Christ. Lent can begin as early as February 4 or as late as March 10. Because of the variation, a large number of feast days may fall during the season. But there are only four major ones. Here is a little background on these feasts to help you celebrate them in the home.

Feast of the Chair of Saint Peter, Apostle
February 22

The early Church celebrated two different feasts for Peter, one commemorating the day Peter held his first service in Rome, the other celebrating the establishment of the Church in Antioch. In both places, the chair he used to celebrate was venerated.

But the feast is more about the person who occupied the chair than the chair itself. On this day, we thank God for entrusting Saint Peter and his successors with the task of shepherding the Church.

For the Children

It seems odd to celebrate a feast in honor of a chair. But it's not so much about the chair as it is what the chair symbolizes. This feast is our way of honoring Saint Peter as our first Pope. Jesus said, "You are Peter, and on this rock I will build my Church." In other words, he put Peter in charge of the Church. Later we started calling the person in charge the Pope. We also call him the "Bishop of Rome." Ever since Saint Peter, every pope and every bishop has a special chair in his cathedral church. When we celebrate the Chair of Peter, the Apostle, we are celebrating our unity as a Church.

Feast of Saint Patrick
March 17

Saint Patrick's Day began as a holy day but morphed into more of a cultural event than a religious one. Nonetheless, the holiday is a celebration of Patrick of Ireland, the son of a Roman soldier who was captured and sold into slavery in Ireland. After six years, he escaped and joined a monastery. Later, when he became a bishop, he returned to Ireland and converted the pagans to Christianity. Legend says he drove all the snakes out of Ireland. The shamrock came to be associated with this feast because Patrick used its three leaves to explain the concept of the Trinity: three parts, one stem; three Persons, one God.

For the Children

Saint Patrick's Day is a really important feast for the Irish. Patrick was the son of a Roman soldier who was caught and made a slave in Ireland. Later, he escaped and became a monk. He came back to Ireland to teach the Irish about God. He used the shamrock to explain how God the Father, Son, and Spirit were three Persons, even though they were one God—just like the shamrock has three bumps, but all of them are part of one leaf.

Let's make some shamrocks and put them on our Easter Tree.

Solemnity of Saint Joseph, Husband of Mary
March 19

Not all feasts are of equal importance. The feast of Saint Joseph, husband of Mary, is a solemnity. A solemnity is the most important kind of feast, reserved for very special people and events. Daily Mass on these days feels more like Sunday Mass, including the Gloria and the Creed, which are left out of lesser feasts.

A solemnity is so important, in fact, that we are excused from Lenten fasting and abstinence on those days. Of course, this doesn't mean we should forget the season and act like it's time to indulge in everything we gave up. But it is a feast worth celebrating.

Saint Joseph, the earthly father of Jesus, doesn't have a large presence in Scripture, but what is there shows him to be a faithful man and protector of Mary and the child Jesus. One legend says Mary had many admirers. All of them left a staff in the temple one night so that God could indicate whom she should marry; Joseph's staff blossomed with white flowers. This is why most statues of Saint Joseph depict him holding a stalk of white lilies. His role as protector of the Mother of God led Joseph to be named the patron and protector of the worldwide Church.

This feast is a big deal in Italy, where people were saved from a famine in the Middle Ages through his intercession. Often, the feast is observed with a community meal, and the poor and needy are invited to share. If you don't feel up to organizing a community event, try observing the feast at home.

Prepare a Saint Joseph table (*tavola di San Giuseppe)*, decorated with a sprig of lilies and spread with meatless dishes like stuffed artichokes, pasta, seafood, and minestrone soup, as well as breads, cookies, and pastries. Rather than using parmesan cheese, heat some bread crumbs in olive oil to symbolize the sawdust from Saint Joseph's floor.

For the Children

Saint Joseph's feast is a very important one because Joseph had to take care of Jesus when he was a child growing up.

Solemnity of the Annunciation
March 25

Annunciation. This is a big word for kids; be sure to explain to them that it comes from the word *announce* and that it's the day the angel Gabriel came to visit Mary. Notice that the date is exactly nine months before Christmas. This is done to tie the two days together.

In the Eastern Church, Mary is called "Theotokos," which literally means *God-bearer,* or *the one who gives birth to God.* Mary is important, not only because she gave birth to Jesus, but because she is the "new Eve." Like her predecessor in the Garden of Eden, Mary had a choice to make. But unlike Eve, she chose obedience and trust in God. Mary, then, helped bring about our salvation.

Since it is a solemnity, celebrate with a special meal. This might be a good time to serve an angel food cake, in honor of Gabriel. Another traditional food for feast days is waffles. Serve them with all the fixings to make the day special.

For the Children

Mary goes by lots of names in the Catholic Church. One of those is the "new Eve." In the Garden of Eden, Eve had the chance to say yes to God and no to evil, but she didn't. And all people since then have been slaves to sin. But Mary said yes to God, and so we honor her for being the one to bring Jesus into the world as a human being.

Appendix B · Patterns for Your Easter Tree

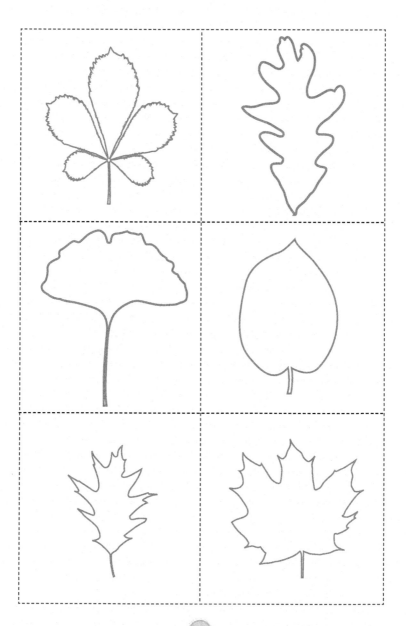

Appendix B · Patterns for Your Easter Tree